Essential Words

for Middle-Grade Students

By
DEBORAH WHITE BROADWATER

COPYRIGHT © 2002 Mark Twain Media, Inc.

ISBN 1-58037-201-5

Printing No. CD-1547

Mark Twain Media, Inc., Publishers
Distributed by Carson-Dellosa Publishing Company, Inc.

Table of Contents

Science

Careers

Etiquette

Character Building

Everyday Words

Recreation

CONSUMER MANAGEMENT

Technology

Writing

Introduction to the Teacher

It is important for students to continually work at improving their vocabularies. As they get older and communicate more with others, they need to have a vast vocabulary to help them with that communication.

This book is intended to offer both the teacher and the parent lessons to help the student improve and enrich his or her vocabulary. For each unit in this book, there is a list of vocabulary words and the category in which they may fit. The list is then divided into four sections to allow the students to concentrate on a manageable number of words at one time. Most sections feature a page where students look up the meaning of the vocabulary word and write a sentence to go with the word. This also helps the student practice dictionary skills. These pages may be copied so the student can keep them in a three-ring binder to use as a resource when he or she is writing. Each section also has skill pages where the student will use the vocabulary words just learned. Some sections include questions about the vocabulary or short writing pieces in which to practice the new vocabulary words.

Teachers may use these activities when teaching vocabulary to the whole class as part of a writing workshop. They may also use these activities for students interested in improving their vocabularies as an enrichment activity.

Each unit can be used in order, or the units can be used in isolation.

Improving Your Vocabulary

The two ways to improve vocabulary are to read and write.

In reading, you need to challenge yourself and read as much and as often as you can. The more you read and the more challenging the books, the more new vocabulary you will encounter.

When you come to a new vocabulary word in your reading, there are several things you can do. Try to pronounce the word. Once you have the word sounded out, it may be a word that you have heard before and know the meaning of, but you have just not seen it in print. Look at the parts of the word; are there clues to the meaning from the base word and the prefixes and suffixes? You can also look for context clues to the meaning of the word. What have you been reading about; do the other words in the sentence help you with the meaning? Perhaps the information that came before this word is helpful. Look at the pictures, if it is a nonfiction book with pictures, and see if they help you figure out the meaning. Try the dictionary or glossary in the book. Sometimes there are endnotes to help you pronounce the word and tell the meaning of the word.

When you come to new vocabulary words in reading, keep a journal of these new words with the meanings of the words. Try to use each new word several times in conversation and in your writing. This journal would also be a great place to keep new and unusual vocabulary words that you hear. Write each one down, so when you have time to look up the definitions, you can include the meaning of each word.

Writing is another way to improve your vocabulary. The more you write, the more your vocabulary will grow. You will soon see that to have a well-written paper, you will need to know strong, interesting, and rich vocabulary words. Your writing will not be as interesting if you continue to use *a lot, very, really,* and *things* when there are many more specific and interesting vocabulary words to use. You can find words to substitute for overused words through your own word list or from a thesaurus.

It is important to communicate well with others. Having a large, interesting vocabulary will help you to accomplish this.

Occupations and Careers: *Vocabulary List*

An occupation or career is the job you plan or hope to have as you get older. Some occupations require a college degree, and some do not. In some occupations, employees receive on-the-job training. Training for other types of jobs is available at technical schools. There are many occupations that require even more than four years of college. It is necessary to get specialized training or a graduate degree to be qualified for some careers.

secretary	gardener	ecologist	computerist
reporter	diva	computer programmer	surgeon
engineer	accountant	dental hygienist	mathematician
chef	firefighter	veterinarian	construction worker
teacher	mechanic	physician	undertaker
lawyer	principal	cartographer	optometrist
salesperson	waitress	geologist	vendor
nurse	executive	architect	professor
doctor	pilot	psychiatrist	photographer
forest ranger	waiter	maitre d'	decorator
dentist	nanny	actor	pharmacist
farmer	sailor	stockbroker	artisan
police officer			auctioneer

3

Name: _____ Date: _____

Occupations and Careers 1: *Matching*

Directions: Match each of the following words with its definition. Write the word in the blank. Use a dictionary if necessary.

secretary	dentist	engineer	reporter	chef
teacher	nurse	doctor	farmer	lawyer
salesperson	forest ranger	police officer		

1. _____ a person who cultivates land and grows crops

2. _____ a person in charge of enforcing the laws of the area

3. _____ a person employed to sell goods

4. _____ a person who gives legal advice to clients

5. _____ a person trained to care for the sick

6. _____ a person who practices medicine as a physician, dentist, or veterinarian

7. _____ a person trained and skilled in an area of engineering

8. _____ a person who takes care of clerical work and correspondence for an organization

9. _____ a doctor who deals with teeth

10. _____ a person who gathers news and writes about it

11. _____ the chief cook

12. _____ a person who is hired by a school to instruct students

13. _____ a person who works for the government to supervise the wooded areas

Name: _____ Date: _____

Occupations and Careers 1: *Sentences*

Directions: Complete the following sentences using the correct word.

secretary	dentist	engineer	reporter	chef
teacher	nurse	doctor	farmer	lawyer
salesperson	forest ranger	police officer		

1. The _____ stood in front of the class and took attendance.

2. I asked the _____ how much the earrings cost.

3. The _____ stopped the speeding car.

4. Did the _____ listen to your lungs with a stethoscope?

5. I asked the school _____ if I could talk to the principal.

6. The _____ at the restaurant wore a big white hat.

7. Jeff said a _____ would defend the criminal in court.

8. Sarah is a _____ and watches for fires in the woods from a tower.

9. A _____ for the local paper came and interviewed our class.

10. Our _____ at school does vision and hearing tests.

11. How many acres of land can the _____ plow in one day?

12. Did an _____ draw the plans for the new electrical system?

13. Laura had an appointment with her _____ to get her teeth cleaned.

Which occupations do you think could be grouped together? Why?

_____

_____

_____

_____

_____

Name: _____ Date: _____

Occupations and Careers 2: *Matching*

Directions: Match the following careers with their definitions.

executive	waitress	principal	gardener	mechanic
firefighter	accountant	nanny	waiter	pilot
sailor	diva			

1. _____ a person with financial skills

2. _____ a person who fights fires

3. _____ a person who takes care of lawns and flower beds

4. _____ a man who serves customers in a restaurant

5. _____ a person licensed to fly an airplane

6. _____ a person who takes care of children

7. _____ the head of a school

8. _____ a person who navigates or operates a boat

9. _____ a leading woman singer, especially in an opera

10. _____ a woman who serves customers in a restaurant

11. _____ a person of authority who works for a business

12. _____ a person who repairs machinery

Can both men and women work in these occupations? Why or why not?

_____

_____

_____

_____

_____

Name: _____ Date: _____

Occupations and Careers 2: *Sentences*

Directions: Complete the following sentences using the correct word.

executives	**waitress**	**principal**	**gardener**	**mechanic**
firefighter	**accountant**	**nanny**	**waiter**	**pilot**
sailor	**diva**			

1. The little girl's _____ took her to the park every day.

2. Dad said that it was time to take the car in to the _____ for a tune-up.

3. Not all _____ work in an office building; some work in their homes.

4. Michelle would like to be an _____ and work with numbers.

5. The _____ at our school makes the morning announcements.

6. Kevin, our _____, took the dinner orders from everyone at the table.

7. Todd is the _____ who drives the hook-and-ladder truck.

8. The _____ of our plane told us to look out the window at the water-fall.

9. The singer was considered a _____ in the opera world.

10. Anna joined the Navy and is now a _____ on an aircraft carrier.

11. A _____ must work very hard all spring and summer to keep the flowers looking beautiful.

12. Midori just got her first job working in a restaurant as a _____.

Which of these occupations are you interested in? Why?

_____

_____

_____

_____

Name: _____ Date: _____

Occupations and Careers 3: *Definitions*

Directions: Use a dictionary to look up the definitions of the following careers. Write a short definition, and then write a sentence that goes with the definition.

1. ecologist _____

   _____

2. computer programmer _____

   _____

3. dental hygienist _____

   _____

4. veterinarian _____

   _____

5. physician _____

   _____

6. cartographer _____

   _____

7. geologist _____

   _____

8. architect _____

   _____

9. psychiatrist _____

   _____

10. maitre d' _____

    _____

11. actor _____

    _____

12. stockbroker _____

    _____

Name: _____ Date: _____

Occupations and Careers 3: *Sentences*

Directions: Complete the following sentences using the correct word.

veterinarian **physician** **cartographer** **ecologist** **architect**
geologist **psychiatrist** **maitre d'** **actor** **stockbrokers**
computer programmer **dental hygienists**

1. We took our dog to the _____ to get her rabies shot.

2. The _____ needed to learn his lines for the play.

3. Dr. Sambula counsels his patients; he is a _____.

4. Dr. McClean has several _____ who clean patients' teeth.

5. Mr. Klimstra is a _____ who studies rocks for a sand company.

6. My brother is a _____ and draws maps for the army.

7. Mrs. Evans is an _____; she works to keep the forest healthy.

8. We wouldn't be able to play computer games if it weren't for a _____.

9. The _____ listened to my lungs in his office.

10. The _____ at the restaurant showed us to our table.

11. _____ buy and sell stocks for people.

12. When our family decided to build our house, we went to an _____ for the plans.

Which of these occupations can be grouped together? Why?

_____

_____

_____

_____

Name: _____ Date: _____

Occupations and Careers 4: *Definitions*

Directions: Use a dictionary to look up the definitions of the following careers. Write a short definition, and then write a sentence that goes with the definition.

1. computerist _____

_____

2. surgeon _____

_____

3. mathematician _____

_____

4. construction worker _____

_____

5. undertaker _____

_____

6. optometrist _____

_____

7. vendor _____

_____

8. professor _____

_____

9. photographer _____

_____

10. decorator _____

_____

11. pharmacist _____

_____

12. artisan _____

_____

13. auctioneer _____

_____

Name: _____   Date: _____

Occupations and Careers 4: *Sentences*

Directions: Complete the following sentences using the correct word.

decorator	surgeon	auctioneer	undertaker	mathematician
optometrist	pharmacist	vendors	photographer	computerist
professor	artisans	construction workers		

1. The _____ works with numbers all day long.

2. Mr. Jeffries is a _____ at State University.

3. According to legend, the _____ was a very busy person in the Wild West.

4. The _____ comes to school every fall to take pictures for the year-book.

5. Bill loves to work with computers; he is a _____.

6. Dr. Hubble, the _____, operated to remove my tonsils.

7. At the school fair, there were many _____ selling books and sup-plies.

8. Many _____ show their work at art fairs.

9. Kendra hopes that one day she will be able to talk as fast as the _____ at the antique sale.

10. In order to get your prescription filled, you need to go to a _____.

11. Dr. Li is an _____; he checked my eyes before school began.

12. My mom and dad are having a _____ come to the house to make suggestions on painting the living room.

13. The new highway will be built by many _____.

Name: _____ Date: _____

Occupations and Careers: *Word Search*

Directions: Find and circle the words listed below in the word search puzzle.

```
X R E K A T R E D N U Z T S I R T A I H C Y S P
O P T O M E T R I S T P R E E N O I T C U A D H
K L M Q Q M K I D E R T I A M E T W A I Q I F Y
T R E M M A R G O R P R E T U P M O C N V Q S S
Y M T S I R E T U P M O C T O S U S V A U E D I
F V M I W R E N E D R A G B A L A D S H M C J C
V E T E R I N A R I A N W I G B I D A C T O R I
P R O F E S S O R P I R L P Z Q W P R E L L W A
P F D T E E D C A R T O G R A P H E R M A O O N
H V Y R U N E R H K R T C E T I H C R A P G G I
A J G O Q G N R E C I F F O E C I L O P I I F U
R F M D K I T X S S E R T I A W G U M H C S A G
M O X N D N I S Q F A R M E R M G A U O N T T E
A R R E M E S R F F S U R G E O N R V T I E A O
C E E V C E T E R E T H G I F E R I F O R X Z L
I S Y K P R H R O T A R O C E D K A N G P E Z O
S T W S E C R E T A R Y P N I G B O A R W C E G
T R A S A L E S P E R S O N U R S E S A U U M I
H A L G B T N A T N U O C C A W W L I P H T D S
X N O H Z P R E K O R B K C O T S T T H Z I O T
C G V N A I C I T A M E H T A M E C R E H V C N
D E N T A L H Y G I E N I S T R T Y A R W E T C
Y R Y F K W R E K R O W N O I T C U R T S N O C
C T E A C H E R E P O R T E R Y N N A N O F R E
```

secretary	forest ranger	undertaker	reporter	computer programmer
mechanic	nurse	veterinarian	engineer	mathematician
physician	cartographer	chef	principal	geologist
dentist	gardener	waitress	architect	maitre d'
diva	farmer	actor	stockbroker	teacher
executive	optometrist	vendor	lawyer	police officer
pharmacist	photographer	accountant	nanny	decorator
surgeon	firefighter	waiter	ecologist	computerist
salesperson	pilot	auctioneer	psychiatrist	dental hygienist
sailor	professor	artisan	doctor	construction worker

Character Building: *Vocabulary List*

It is important to use words that will help you build not only your vocabulary, but also your character. Think of these words as important traits to look for in other people and also as words to try to keep in your life. A good, strong character will be a great asset to you as you go through life.

respect	graceful	esteem	genial
optimism	careful	hospitable	integrity
honest	creative	attribute	distinguished
fortitude	championship	temperament	propriety
caring	kindness	competency	gallant
mannerly	civil	visionary	persuasive
polite	concern	reason	insightful
loyalty	reputation	discerning	adaptable
personality	sociable	aristocratic	experienced
responsibility	dependable	tireless	resolute
confidence	resourceful	attentive	attitude
trustworthy	humane	conviction	ethical
	vigor	compassion	

Name: _____ Date: _____

Character Building 1: *Definitions*

Directions: Use a dictionary to look up the definitions of the following character-building words. Write a short definition, and then write a sentence that goes with the definition.

1. loyalty _____

_____

2. responsibility _____

_____

3. polite _____

_____

4. personality _____

_____

5. respect _____

_____

6. mannerly _____

_____

7. optimism _____

_____

8. confidence _____

_____

9. trustworthy _____

_____

10. fortitude _____

_____

11. honest _____

_____

12. caring _____

_____

Name: _____ Date: _____

Character Building 1: *Sentences/Synonyms*

Directions: Fill in the blank with the correct character-building vocabulary word.

polite   respect   honest   confidence   caring   responsibility

1. Joelle talked back to the teacher; she did not show him much _____.

2. My mom said she had the utmost _____ in me and knew I would do well on the test.

3. The student council members have a lot of _____ in making sure they get all the information back to the students.

4. Abraham Lincoln was thought of as a very _____ person.

5. In order to be a nurse, you must be a _____ person.

6. Steven was extremely _____ when he offered to carry Mrs. Jenkins' groceries.

Directions: Write two synonyms for the following vocabulary words. Use a dictionary or thesaurus if you need help.

1. mannerly   _____   _____

2. fortitude   _____   _____

3. personality   _____   _____

4. trustworthy   _____   _____

5. optimism   _____   _____

6. loyalty   _____   _____

Directions: Write a paragraph using four of the vocabulary words from this page. Underline the vocabulary words you use.

_____

_____

_____

_____

_____

Name: _____ Date: _____

Character Building 2: *Definitions*

Directions: Use a dictionary to look up the definitions of the following character-building words. Write a short definition, and then write a sentence that goes with the definition.

1. vigor _____

   _____

2. championship _____

   _____

3. humane _____

   _____

4. kindness _____

   _____

5. resourceful _____

   _____

6. reputation _____

   _____

7. creative _____

   _____

8. sociable _____

   _____

9. careful _____

   _____

10. dependable _____

   _____

11. graceful _____

   _____

12. civil _____

   _____

13. concern _____

   _____

Name: _____ Date: _____

Character Building 2: *Sentences/Synonyms*

Directions: Fill in the blank with the correct vocabulary word.

kindness   careful   concern   humane   championship   sociable   reputation

1. Please be _____ with the fire, so you don't get burned.

2. Luis showed much _____ toward his little sister when he fixed her

   broken toy.

3. We won the state _____ in volleyball.

4. The dogcatcher took the dogs to the _____ Society.

5. Mrs. Jackson has the _____ of being a fair teacher.

6. You don't have to _____ yourself with my troubles.

7. The new boy is very _____ and gets along with almost everyone.

Directions: Write two synonyms for the following vocabulary words. Use a dictionary or the-saurus if you need help.

1. creative   _____   _____

2. humane   _____   _____

3. civil   _____   _____

4. graceful   _____   _____

5. dependable   _____   _____

6. resourceful   _____   _____

7. vigor   _____   _____

Directions: Write a paragraph using five of the vocabulary words from this page. Underline the vocabulary words you use.

_____

_____

_____

_____

_____

Name: _____ Date: _____

Character Building 3: *Definitions*

Directions: Use a dictionary to look up the definitions of the following character-building words. Write a short definition, and then write a sentence that goes with the definition.

1. tireless _____

   _____

2. esteem _____

   _____

3. aristocratic _____

   _____

4. compassion _____

   _____

5. discerning _____

   _____

6. hospitable _____

   _____

7. reason _____

   _____

8. attentive _____

   _____

9. visionary _____

   _____

10. conviction _____

    _____

11. competency _____

    _____

12. attribute _____

    _____

13. temperament _____

    _____

Name: _____ Date: _____

Character Building 3: *Matching/Synonyms/Antonyms*

Directions: Fill in each blank with the correct vocabulary word.

| **temperament** | **hospitable** | **esteem** | **conviction** | **aristocratic** | **visionary** |

1. _____ having foresight

2. _____ to respect or hold in high regard

3. _____ a firm belief

4. _____ having qualities of high society

5. _____ a person's personality

6. _____ welcoming to people

Directions: Write one synonym and one antonym for each of the following words. Use a dictionary or thesaurus if you need help.

	Synonyms	**Antonyms**
1. reason	_____	_____
2. attentive	_____	_____
3. competency	_____	_____
4. discerning	_____	_____
5. tireless	_____	_____
6. attribute	_____	_____
7. compassion	_____	_____

Directions: Using three of the vocabulary words from this page, write a sentence for each one. Underline the vocabulary word in each sentence.

1. _____

2. _____

3. _____

Name: _____ Date: _____

Character Building 4: *Definitions*

Directions: Use a dictionary to look up the definitions of the following character-building words. Write a short definition, and then write a sentence that goes with the definition.

1. insightful _____

    _____

2. attitude _____

    _____

3. persuasive _____

    _____

4. genial _____

    _____

5. adaptable _____

    _____

6. integrity _____

    _____

7. resolute _____

    _____

8. distinguished _____

    _____

9. gallant _____

    _____

10. propriety _____

    _____

11. ethical _____

    _____

12. experienced _____

    _____

Name: _____ Date: _____

Character Building 4: *Sentences/Synonyms/Antonyms/ Short Answers*

Directions: Fill in the blank with the correct vocabulary word.

genial   distinguished   persuasive   resolute   attitude

1. My grandfather thinks his gray hair makes him look _____.

2. To do well in school, you must work hard, and you need a good _____.

3. Scott's speech was very _____, and I voted for him for treasurer.

4. Lauren's disposition is _____; she always has a smile.

5. Mike was _____ in his decision not to try smoking.

Directions: Write a synonym and an antonym for each of the following words. Use a dictionary or thesaurus if you need help.

	Synonyms	**Antonyms**
1. adaptable	_____	_____
2. ethical	_____	_____
3. integrity	_____	_____
4. propriety	_____	_____
5. gallant	_____	_____

Directions: Answer the following questions. Use a dictionary if you need help.

1. Do you need glasses to be **insightful**? _____

   Why or why not? _____

   _____

2. If you are new to a job, are you **experienced**? _____

   Why or why not? _____

   _____

Name: _____ Date: _____

Character Building: *Crossword Puzzle*

Directions: Use the clues below to complete the crossword puzzle.

ACROSS

1. The quality of caring about others
5. Conforming to moral standards
6. Showing the best qualities of humankind, such as sympathy and kindness
7. Accountability
10. Truthful
13. Showing good manners
15. To respect or hold in high regard
16. Imaginative or inventive
17. Reliable; trustworthy
18. Having the power to convince or sway someone's opinion

DOWN

2. Considerate of others
3. The quality of faithfulness to a person or idea
4. Cheerful; friendly
7. To show esteem for someone
8. The quality of being of sound moral principal; uprightness
9. Strength to endure
11. Showing the ability to understand the inner nature of things
12. Having the ability to speak well
14. Having a fixed purpose; determined
16. Polite or courteous, especially in a formal manner

Everyday Words: *Vocabulary List*

There are words that you see in your everyday life that may be new vocabulary words to you. It is important to learn these words and what they mean so you will be able to read and understand instructions, newspapers, and other printed materials. These words are also important for understanding the news and other television programs. Some of the words you may already know, and some may be new.

composite	situation	environment	beneficial
biopsy	escort	colleague	rampage
dowdy	resource	zealous	negligible
apparatus	ecological	jubilant	personable
fervor	fertile	calligraphy	arbitrary
align	terrarium	extemporaneous	retort
academic	seminar	debonair	jargon
impromptu	shun	eloquent	prudent
disheveled	junction	inhumane	complacent
enviable	adept	meander	frugal
refuse	delegate	orchestrate	judicial
remote	linger	paraphrase	saunter
	commence	candor	

Name: _____ Date: _____

Everyday Words 1: *Definitions*

Directions: Use a dictionary to look up the definitions of the following everyday words. Write a short definition, and then write a sentence that goes with the definition.

1. composite _____

   _____

2. refuse _____

   _____

3. remote _____

   _____

4. enviable _____

   _____

5. biopsy _____

   _____

6. disheveled _____

   _____

7. impromptu _____

   _____

8. academic _____

   _____

9. dowdy _____

   _____

10. align _____

    _____

11. fervor _____

    _____

12. apparatus _____

    _____

Name: _____ Date: _____

Everyday Words 1: *Matching/Short Answers*

Directions: Fill in the blank with the correct vocabulary word.

dowdy   **enviable**   **biopsy**   **refuse**   **composite**   **academic**

1. _____ made up of several components

2. _____ not stylish

3. _____ trash

4. _____ desired

5. _____ pertaining to a school

6. _____ tissue removed from the body to test for disease

Directions: Answer each of the following questions. Use a dictionary if you need help.

1. Can you use an **apparatus** for gymnastics? _____

   Why or why not? _____

2. Would your hair be combed if you were **disheveled**? _____

   Why or why not? _____

3. Can you use a pencil to **align**? _____

   Why or why not? _____

4. If you are in the Arctic, are you in a **remote** area?

   Why or why not? _____

5. Has an **impromptu** speech been well rehearsed?

   Why or why not? _____

6. Does someone who has a warm forehead have a **fervor**?

   Why or why not? _____

Name: _____ Date: _____

Everyday Words 2: *Definitions*

Directions: Use a dictionary to look up the definitions of the following everyday words. Write a short definition, and then write a sentence that goes with the definition.

1. situation _____
   _____

2. linger _____
   _____

3. escort _____
   _____

4. delegate _____
   _____

5. resource _____
   _____

6. adept _____
   _____

7. ecological _____
   _____

8. commence _____
   _____

9. fertile _____
   _____

10. junction _____
    _____

11. terrarium _____
    _____

12. shun _____
    _____

13. seminar _____
    _____

Name: _____ Date: _____

Everyday Words 2: *Sentences/Matching/Short Answers*

Directions: Complete the following sentences using the correct word.

ecological	shun	fertile	escort	seminar	terrarium
resource					

1. Jason was told to _____ chocolate because he is allergic to it.

2. In college, students may study a subject in a _____.

3. Annie keeps her newt in a _____ with some plants.

4. The Midwest is a _____ farming area.

5. Our class recycles cans as an _____ project.

6. Coal is considered a natural _____.

7. Ben was to _____ Mrs. Jones to the podium.

Directions: Fill in the blank with the correct vocabulary word.

junction	situation	delegate	linger	commence	adept

1. _____ location or position

2. _____ someone who represents someone or something

3. _____ to wait or remain behind

4. _____ to be skilled

5. _____ begin

6. _____ intersection

Directions: Answer each of the following questions. Use a dictionary if you need help.

1. Could a **delegate** be in Congress? _____

   Why or why not? _____

2. Does the **shun** set in the west? _____

   Why or why not? _____

Name: _____ Date: _____

Everyday Words 3: *Definitions*

Directions: Use a dictionary to look up the definitions of the following everyday words. Write a short definition, and then write a sentence that goes with the definition.

1. candor _____

   _____

2. environment _____

   _____

3. paraphrase _____

   _____

4. colleague _____

   _____

5. orchestrate _____

   _____

6. zealous _____

   _____

7. meander _____

   _____

8. jubilant _____

   _____

9. inhumane _____

   _____

10. calligraphy _____

    _____

11. eloquent _____

    _____

12. extemporaneous _____

    _____

13. debonair _____

    _____

Name: _____ Date: _____

Everyday Words 3: *Matching/Synonyms/Antonyms/Short Answers*

Directions: Fill in each blank with the correct vocabulary word.

calligraphy   **paraphrase**   **orchestrate**   **debonair**   **environment**   **inhumane**

1. _____ surroundings

2. _____ fancy, decorative writing

3. _____ lacking compassion

4. _____ to lead or organize

5. _____ to put in other words

6. _____ well-dressed; suave

Directions: Write one synonym and one antonym for each of the following words. Use a dictionary or thesaurus if you need help.

	Synonyms	Antonyms
1. colleague	_____	_____
2. candor	_____	_____
3. eloquent	_____	_____
4. extemporaneous	_____	_____
5. jubilant	_____	_____
6. zealous	_____	_____
7. meander	_____	_____

Directions: Answer each of the following questions. Use a dictionary if you need help.

1. Do you use a **candor** to open a can? _____

   Why or why not? _____

2. Can a stream **meander** through the woodlands? _____

   Why or why not? _____

Name: _____ Date: _____

Everyday Words 4: *Definitions*

Directions: Use a dictionary to look up the definitions of the following everyday words. Write a short definition, and then write a sentence that goes with the definition.

1. saunter _____

   _____

2. beneficial _____

   _____

3. judicial _____

   _____

4. rampage _____

   _____

5. frugal _____

   _____

6. negligible _____

   _____

7. complacent _____

   _____

8. personable _____

   _____

9. prudent _____

   _____

10. arbitrary _____

    _____

11. jargon _____

    _____

12. retort _____

    _____

Name: _____ Date: _____

Everyday Words 4: *Sentences/Synonyms/Antonyms/Short Answers*

Directions: Fill in each blank with the correct vocabulary word.

rampage   retort   complacent   frugal   negligible   beneficial

1. Stefano gave Mrs. Cortez a snappy _____ to the question of the day.

2. The wild deer was on a _____ when it was cornered in the store.

3. My dad said I need to be more _____ and save some money.

4. Barb said studying for the test would be _____ to us and our grades.

5. Michael said we received only a _____ amount of rain.

6. When your grades are high, don't become _____ and slack off.

Directions: Write one synonym and one antonym for each of the following words. Use a dictionary or thesaurus if you need help.

	Synonyms	**Antonyms**
1. personable	_____	_____
2. saunter	_____	_____
3. arbitrary	_____	_____
4. jargon	_____	_____
5. judicial	_____	_____
6. prudent	_____	_____

Directions: Answer each of the following questions. Use a dictionary if you need help.

1. If the rope is loose, do you need to **retort** it? _____

   Why or why not? _____

2. Do some professions have a special **jargon** to communicate with each other? _____

   Why or why not? _____

Words to Enrich Writing: *Vocabulary List*

When you are writing papers or letters, you should use your best vocabulary. Instead of using words like *neat* or *a lot*, it is important to think about words that convey the meaning you want. When you are specific in your choice of words, the reader knows exactly what you want to say. You should also think about the adverbs and adjectives that you use. Think of specific words instead of *very* or *really*. There are many words that can be used to enrich your writing.

important	trying	eloquence	somber
sadness	enjoyable	evict	fictitious
uneventful	sorrowful	habitat	browse
excited	reserved	temporary	deteriorate
shy	awkward	vivacious	inclination
gloomy	radiant	reluctant	extinguish
hopeless	enormous	momentary	overjoyed
colorful	pale	squander	generality
unusual	constrained	clarify	imminent
elated	impeccable	allude	elaboration
shimmer	alleged	opportunity	desire
encroach	impressive	enlighten	multitude
	sparkle	bellow	

32

Name: _____ Date: _____

Words to Enrich Writing 1: *Definitions*

Directions: Use a dictionary to look up the definitions of the following words to enrich writing. Write a short definition, and then write a sentence that goes with the definition.

1. shimmer _____

   _____

2. elated _____

   _____

3. encroach _____

   _____

4. unusual _____

   _____

5. important _____

   _____

6. colorful _____

   _____

7. sadness _____

   _____

8. hopeless _____

   _____

9. uneventful _____

   _____

10. gloomy _____

    _____

11. excited _____

    _____

12. shy _____

    _____

Name: _____ Date: _____

Words to Enrich Writing 1: *Matching/Antonyms*

Directions: Fill in the blank with the correct vocabulary word.

| shimmer | sadness | uneventful | hopeless | excited | encroach |

1. _____ to gradually move forward

2. _____ to reflect light

3. _____ having one's emotions aroused

4. _____ desperate

5. _____ ordinary or routine

6. _____ unhappiness

Directions: Write two antonyms for the following vocabulary words. Use a dictionary or thesaurus if you need help.

1. gloomy _____ _____

2. colorful _____ _____

3. elated _____ _____

4. important _____ _____

5. unusual _____ _____

6. shy _____ _____

Directions: Use five of the words to enrich vocabulary from this page to write a descriptive paragraph. Add five of your own words. Underline the vocabulary words you use.

_____

_____

_____

_____

_____

_____

Name: _____   Date: _____

Words to Enrich Writing 2: *Definitions*

Directions: Use a dictionary to look up the definitions of the following words to enrich writing. Write a short definition, and then write a sentence that goes with the definition.

1. sparkle _____

    _____

2. alleged _____

    _____

3. impeccable _____

    _____

4. impressive _____

    _____

5. constrained _____

    _____

6. enjoyable _____

    _____

7. pale _____

    _____

8. sorrowful _____

    _____

9. enormous _____

    _____

10. reserved _____

    _____

11. radiant _____

    _____

12. awkward _____

    _____

13. trying _____

    _____

Name: _____ Date: _____

Words to Enrich Writing 2: *Sentences/Synonyms*

Directions: Complete the following sentences with the correct vocabulary word.

alleged   reserved   impressive   sparkled   trying   pale

1. The shy, _____ girl sat alone at the party.

2. The daffodil was a _____ yellow color.

3. Jennifer's eyes _____ as she opened the present.

4. Carol's excellent horsemanship looked _____ to the judges.

5. Mother told the twins that they were _____ her patience.

6. The _____ bank robber was brought to trial.

Directions: Write two synonyms for the following vocabulary words. Use a dictionary or thesaurus if you need help.

1. enormous   _____   _____

2. impeccable   _____   _____

3. sorrowful   _____   _____

4. constrained   _____   _____

5. enjoyable   _____   _____

6. awkward   _____   _____

7. radiant   _____   _____

Directions: Use six of the vocabulary words from this page to write a descriptive paragraph. Underline the vocabulary words you use.

_____

_____

_____

_____

_____

_____

Name: _____ Date: _____

Words to Enrich Writing 3: *Definitions*

Directions: Use a dictionary to look up the definitions of the following words to enrich writing. Write a short definition, and then write a sentence that goes with the definition.

1. evict _____
_____

2. opportunity _____
_____

3. allude _____
_____

4. temporary _____
_____

5. squander _____
_____

6. clarify _____
_____

7. habitat _____
_____

8. eloquence _____
_____

9. vivacious _____
_____

10. reluctant _____
_____

11. momentary _____
_____

12. bellow _____
_____

13. enlighten _____
_____

Name: _____ Date: _____

Words to Enrich Writing 3: *Sentences/Matching*

Directions: Complete the following sentences with the correct vocabulary word.

enlighten   temporary   opportunity   squander   momentary   evict

1. I lost my library card, so the librarian gave me a _____ one until I found mine.

2. Dad tried to _____ the bird from the house, chasing it with a broom.

3. Mrs. Chen gave us the _____ to try out for the play.

4. Bryan had his allowance, and he wanted to _____ it on comic books.

5. Mr. Brennan was to _____ us on the care of cacti.

6. Juan had a _____ lapse in memory.

Directions: Fill in the blank with the correct vocabulary word.

habitat   allude   bellow   eloquence   reluctant   clarify   vivacious

1. _____ a roar

2. _____ to make something clearer

3. _____ skill in speech or writing

4. _____ to refer to indirectly

5. _____ animated and lively

6. _____ unwilling; holding back

7. _____ something's natural environment

Name: _____ Date: _____

Words to Enrich Writing 4: *Definitions*

Directions: Use a dictionary to look up the definitions of the following words to enrich writing. Write a short definition, and then write a sentence that goes with the definition.

1. overjoyed _____
    _____

2. multitude _____
    _____

3. desire _____
    _____

4. somber _____
    _____

5. elaboration _____
    _____

6. deteriorate _____
    _____

7. fictitious _____
    _____

8. browse _____
    _____

9. generality _____
    _____

10. imminent _____
    _____

11. inclination _____
    _____

12. extinguish _____
    _____

Name: _____ Date: _____

Words to Enrich Writing 4: *Short Answers*

Directions: Answer the following questions. Use a dictionary if you need help.

1. Are you **somber** at a birthday party? _____

   Why or why not? _____

2. Is a story that is **fictitious** made up from imagination? _____

   Why or why not? _____

3. Is an **elaboration** a brief explanation? _____

   Why or why not? _____

4. Do you have **browse** over your eyes? _____

   Why or why not? _____

5. If you see a fire can you **extinguish** it? _____

   Why or why not? _____

6. Would you be **overjoyed** if you won a contest? _____

   Why or why not? _____

7. If you are thirsty, might you **desire** a drink of water? _____

   Why or why not? _____

8. When there is road construction ahead, do you have to **deteriorate**? _____

   Why or why not? _____

Directions: Using two of the vocabulary words from this page, write sentences using each of them correctly. Underline the vocabulary words you use.

_____

_____

_____

_____

Name: _____ Date: _____

Words to Enrich Writing 4: *Review*

Directions: Review the words to enrich writing. On the lines below, write about a favorite time in your life. Use as many of the words as you can. Circle the vocabulary words.

_____

_____

_____

_____

_____

_____

_____

_____

_____

_____

_____

_____

_____

_____

_____

_____

_____

_____

_____

_____

_____

_____

_____

_____

_____

Recreation and Fitness: *Vocabulary List*

Recreation is a big part of everyone's life. There is vocabulary that is specific to this area. Some words may be familiar to you, but others will be new. In order to enrich your vocabulary, it is important to know words from all areas of physical fitness, sports, hobbies, and health.

crunch	backboard	embroidery	aerobics
blocking	court	philatelist	offense
dunk	foul	referee	avocation
fumble	goal post	arena	defense
penalty	triathlete	stamina	craft
coach	fitness	competition	league
angler	croquet	wellness	skeletal
target	badminton	curling	treadmill
ace	carbohydrate	woodworking	Olympian
quiver	barbell	tournament	aviation
agility	endurance	vascular	prestidigitation
bunker	marathon	spectator	gymnast
accelerate			terpsichorean

Name: _____ Date: _____

Recreation and Fitness 1: *Definitions*

Directions: Use a dictionary to look up the definitions of the following recreation and fitness words. Write a short definition, and then write a sentence that goes with the definition.

1. crunch (exercising) _____

   _____

2. accelerate _____

   _____

3. ace _____

   _____

4. bunker (sports) _____

   _____

5. blocking (sports) _____

   _____

6. agility _____

   _____

7. target _____

   _____

8. penalty _____

   _____

9. dunk (sports) _____

   _____

10. coach _____

    _____

11. angler _____

    _____

12. quiver (sports) _____

    _____

13. fumble (sports) _____

    _____

Name: _____ Date: _____

Recreation and Fitness 1: *Synonyms/Story Writing*

Directions: Write a synonym for the following recreation and fitness words. Use a dictionary or thesaurus if you need help.

1. accelerate _____   2. bunker _____

3. agility _____   4. penalty _____

5. ace _____   6. crunch _____

7. coach _____   8. fumble _____

9. dunk _____   10. blocking _____

11. angler _____   12. quiver _____

13. target _____

Directions: On the lines below, use seven of the vocabulary words from this page, and write a story. Underline the vocabulary words.

_____

_____

_____

_____

_____

_____

_____

_____

_____

_____

_____

_____

_____

Name: _____ Date: _____

Recreation and Fitness 2: *Definitions*

Directions: Use a dictionary to look up the definitions of the following recreation and fitness words. Write a short definition, and then write a sentence that goes with the definition.

1. court _____

   _____

2. marathon _____

   _____

3. foul _____

   _____

4. endurance_____

   _____

5. goal post _____

   _____

6. fitness _____

   _____

7. barbell _____

   _____

8. carbohydrate _____

   _____

9. triathlete _____

   _____

10. badminton _____

    _____

11. croquet _____

    _____

12. backboard _____

    _____

Name: _____ Date: _____

Recreation and Fitness 2: *Matching*

Directions: Fill in the blank with the correct vocabulary word.

endurance	**foul**	**badminton**	**marathon**	**croquet**
court	**backboard**	**goal post**	**triathlete**	**fitness**
carbohydrates	**barbell**			

1. _____ the area in basketball that the basket is attached to

2. _____ a 26-mile endurance race

3. _____ a person who competes in a contest with swimming, biking,

    and running

4. _____ a game using a net, a racket, and a shuttlecock

5. _____ the level area used for basketball, tennis, or racquetball

6. _____ starches and sugars important to humans

7. _____ against the rules of a game

8. _____ a lawn game with wickets, wooden balls, and mallets

9. _____ supports a crossbar to form the goal

10. _____ a rod with adjustable weights on the ends

11. _____ health

12. _____ the ability to continue despite fatigue

Name: _____ Date: _____

Recreation and Fitness 2: *Short Answers*

Directions: Answer the following questions. Use a dictionary if you need help.

1. Can you carry a **barbell** in your pocket? _____

   Why or why not? _____

2. Is **fitness** important to your health? _____

   Why or why not? _____

3. Can you touch a **backboard** while standing on your feet? _____

   Why or why not? _____

4. Could one person play **badminton**? _____

   Why or why not? _____

5. Do you need to train for a **marathon**? _____

   Why or why not? _____

6. Can you play **croquet** in the house? _____

   Why or why not? _____

7. Are there hills on a **court**? _____

   Why or why not? _____

8. If you have **endurance**, should you avoid playing sports? _____

   Why or why not? _____

9. To be a **triathlete**, do you need to be able to fish? _____

   Why or why not? _____

10. Is basketball a game with **goal posts**? _____

    Why or why not? _____

Name: _____ Date: _____

Recreation and Fitness 3: *Definitions*

Directions: Use a dictionary to look up the definitions of the following recreation and fitness words. Write a short definition, and then write a sentence that goes with the definition.

1. philatelist _____

   _____

2. referee _____

   _____

3. embroidery _____

   _____

4. arena _____

   _____

5. stamina _____

   _____

6. competition _____

   _____

7. wellness _____

   _____

8. curling _____

   _____

9. woodworking _____

   _____

10. tournament _____

    _____

11. vascular_____

    _____

12. spectator _____

    _____

Name: _____ Date: _____

Recreation and Fitness 3: *Sentences/Synonyms*

Directions: Complete the following sentences with the correct vocabulary word.

curling	wellness	woodworking	vascular
embroidery	philatelist		

1. Kwan likes shop class; he gets to do _____.

2. My grandfather collects stamps; he is a _____.

3. Aunt Cathy has stitched _____ on the edges of the pillowcases.

4. Our health teacher has started a new _____ club where we learn about fitness and nutrition.

5. A game played on ice with a large stone is called _____.

6. You need good _____ health, so your heart works well.

Directions: Write two synonyms for the following vocabulary words. Use a dictionary or thesaurus if you need help.

1. spectator _____ _____

2. referee _____ _____

3. arena _____ _____

4. competition _____ _____

5. stamina _____ _____

6. tournament _____ _____

Do you know anyone whose hobby is woodworking or embroidery? What are some of the items he or she produces? Would you be interested in learning one of these hobbies? Write a descriptive paragraph below about one of these hobbies. Underline any vocabulary words you use.

_____

_____

_____

_____

_____

_____

Name: _____ Date: _____

Recreation and Fitness 3: *Matching*

Directions: Fill in the blank with the correct vocabulary word.

tournament	embroidery	referee	arena	vascular
stamina	philatelist	competition	wellness	curling
woodworking	spectator			

1. _____ about carrying blood through the body

2. _____ the study of health and fitness

3. _____ a person officiating at a sporting event

4. _____ designs on cloth usually made with colored threads

5. _____ a game played on ice with a large stone and brooms

6. _____ a large area or building used for sports

7. _____ a contest for a prize

8. _____ the making of items using wood

9. _____ the power to continue when fatigued

10. _____ a person who watches a sporting event

11. _____ a series of contests or games

12. _____ a person who collects stamps

Directions: Use five of the words from this page to write a descriptive paragraph. Remember to check your spelling. Underline the vocabulary words you use.

_____

_____

_____

_____

_____

_____

50

Name: _____   Date: _____

Recreation and Fitness 4: *Definitions*

Directions: Use a dictionary to look up the definitions of the following recreation and fitness words. Write a short definition, and then write a sentence that goes with the definition.

1. terpsichorean _____

   _____

2. aerobics _____

   _____

3. offense _____

   _____

4. gymnast _____

   _____

5. avocation _____

   _____

6. treadmill _____

   _____

7. prestidigitation _____

   _____

8. defense _____

   _____

9. aviation _____

   _____

10. craft _____

   _____

11. Olympian _____

   _____

12. league _____

   _____

13. skeletal _____

   _____

Name: _____   Date: _____

Recreation and Fitness 4: *Sentences/Synonyms*

Directions: Complete the following sentences with the correct vocabulary word.

offense	**prestidigitation**	**Olympian**	**terpsichorean**
treadmill	**aerobics**		

1. My brother knows _____; he can do magic tricks.

2. Sara has been training for years; she wants to be an _____.

3. Dad set the _____ in his bedroom, so he could get some exercise.

4. Karl plays quarterback on the football team; he plays _____.

5. Our wellness club has started _____ exercises after school.

6. Caroline has _____ talent; she loves to dance.

Directions: Write two synonyms for the following vocabulary words. Use a dictionary or the-saurus if you need help.

1. avocation   _____   _____

2. gymnast   _____   _____

3. craft   _____   _____

4. aviation   _____   _____

5. skeletal   _____   _____

6. league   _____   _____

7. defense   _____   _____

Write two sentences below describing some examples of prestidigitation.

_____

_____

_____

_____

Etiquette: *Vocabulary List*

In today's world, it is important to use good etiquette at all times. Etiquette is the forms, manners, and ceremonies established by conventions as acceptable or required in social relations. In other words, it is the proper way to behave. Whether you are communicating with friends, parents, teachers, or others, make sure that in your speech and writing you are using good etiquette.

invitation	politely	RSVP	deference
please	thank you	chivalrous	boorish
respond	social	aplomb	arrogance
belated	compliment	belligerent	debutante
apologize	tribute	appease	remorseful
curtsy	respectful	cordial	homage
socialite	culture	rueful	genteel
appreciation	courteous	refinement	suave
valiant	thoughtful	apropos	tact
gracious	diplomatic	amenable	obliging
encouragement	formal	affable	hospitality
nicety	correctness	dignity	decorum
	manners	benevolent	

Name: _____ Date: _____

Etiquette 1: *Definitions*

Directions: Use a dictionary to look up the definitions of the following etiquette words. Write a short definition, and then write a sentence that goes with the definition.

1. apologize _____
_____

2. tribute _____
_____

3. socialite _____
_____

4. arrogance _____
_____

5. manners _____
_____

6. respond _____
_____

7. invitation _____
_____

8. thank you _____
_____

9. belated _____
_____

10. respectful _____
_____

11. compliment _____
_____

12. social _____
_____

13. formal _____
_____

Name: _____ Date: _____

Etiquette 1: *Matching*

Directions: Fill in each blank with the correct vocabulary word.

respectful	**social**	**compliment**	**tribute**	**thank you**
formal	**invitation**	**belated**	**arrogance**	**apologize**
socialite	**manners**	**respond**		

1. _____ an expression of gratitude

2. _____ showing politeness

3. _____ dressier than everyday clothes

4. _____ to make an excuse for

5. _____ a written or spoken request to attend an event

6. _____ the polite ways of social behavior

7. _____ a compliment given as respect or admiration

8. _____ an important person in fashionable society

9. _____ a statement of praise

10. _____ coming late

11. _____ to answer; reply

12. _____ a party; having to do with society

13. _____ overbearing pride or self-importance

Directions: Choose five of the vocabulary words from this page, and use them in a paragraph about etiquette. Underline the vocabulary words you use.

_____

_____

_____

_____

_____

Name: _____ Date: _____

Etiquette 2: *Definitions*

Directions: Use a dictionary to look up the definitions of the following etiquette words. Write a short definition, and then write a sentence that goes with the definition.

1. politely _____

   _____

2. correctness _____

   _____

3. culture _____

   _____

4. please _____

   _____

5. appreciation _____

   _____

6. diplomatic _____

   _____

7. nicety _____

   _____

8. encouragement _____

   _____

9. gracious _____

   _____

10. curtsy _____

    _____

11. thoughtful _____

    _____

12. valiant _____

    _____

13. courteous _____

    _____

Name: _____ Date: _____

Etiquette 2: *Sentences*

Directions: Read each sentence. In the blank, write "correct" if the vocabulary word is used correctly, or write "incorrect" if it is used incorrectly.

1. Jamie wrote a **valiant** note to tell his grandparents he liked his present. _____

2. Cassie stood up to be **respectful** when the queen entered the room. _____

3. The balloon **belated** when the air was let out. _____

4. Everyone was yelling **encouragement** as Rick tried to do a pull-up. _____

5. The class wrote a **tribute** to their teacher to be read at the assembly. _____

6. Adam is so **thoughtful**; he always tries to include everyone in the game. _____

7. Did you watch the square dance **social** in the movie about the West? _____

8. I think Kimiko should wear the **nicety** to the dance. _____

9. Betty is going to fill out the application **formal** for the job. _____

10. Mrs. Stevens **complimented** Lakeesha on her outfit. _____

11. How would you properly address the President of the United States?

    _____

12. How would you properly address the governor of your state?

    _____

57

Name: _____ Date: _____

Etiquette 2: *Sentences/Matching/Synonyms/Antonyms*

Directions: Complete each of the following sentences with the correct vocabulary word.

diplomatic	please	curtsy	appreciation	politely

1. Janie asked, "_____, may I have a cookie?"

2. You need to show your _____ when someone does something nice

    for you.

3. The ambassador had to be _____ when talking to the delegates from

    the two feuding countries.

4. Sven _____ asked all the guests to be seated for dinner.

5. "Be sure to _____ when you meet the duchess," said Diana.

Directions: Fill in the blank with the correct vocabulary word.

encouragement	correctness	culture	thoughtful

1. _____ orderliness

2. _____ giving courage, hope, or confidence

3. _____ considerate of others

4. _____ refinement of the intellect, manners, and taste

Directions: Write a synonym and an antonym for each of the following words. Use a dictionary or thesaurus if you need help.

	Synonyms	**Antonyms**
1. gracious	_____	_____
2. nicety	_____	_____
3. courteous	_____	_____
4. valiant	_____	_____

Name: _____ Date: _____

Etiquette 3: *Definitions*

Directions: Use a dictionary to look up the definitions of the following etiquette words. Write a short definition, and then write a sentence that goes with the definition.

1. RSVP _____

   _____

2. cordial _____

   _____

3. tact _____

   _____

4. homage _____

   _____

5. belligerent _____

   _____

6. debutante _____

   _____

7. dignity _____

   _____

8. remorseful _____

   _____

9. chivalrous _____

   _____

10. aplomb _____

    _____

11. benevolent _____

    _____

12. refinement _____

    _____

Name: _____ Date: _____

Etiquette 3: *Sentences/Matching*

Directions: Complete each of the following sentences with the correct vocabulary word.

refinement   **cordial**   **RSVP**   **belligerent**   **benevolent**

1. Charles was _____ and friendly to his guests at the party.

2. When his sister corrected Todd, he became very _____ and difficult

    to deal with.

3. The United Way is a _____ organization; it helps others in the community.

4. Ben's good manners and sophisticated language showed that he had _____.

5. Christy included a request to _____ with her invitations.

Directions: Fill in the blank with the correct vocabulary word.

RSVP	**chivalrous**	**homage**	**debutante**
dignity	**remorseful**	**tact**	**aplomb**

1. _____ courteous to women and girls

2. _____ poise; self-possession

3. _____ full of regret

4. _____ knowing what to say to avoid offending someone

5. _____ self-respect

6. _____ to pay respect or tribute

7. _____ a young lady making her first public appearance in society

8. _____ a reply is requested

Name: _____ Date: _____

Etiquette 4: *Definitions*

Directions: Use a dictionary to look up the definitions of the following etiquette words. Write a short definition, and then write a sentence that goes with the definition.

1. hospitality _____

   _____

2. obliging _____

   _____

3. affable _____

   _____

4. apropos _____

   _____

5. genteel _____

   _____

6. boorish _____

   _____

7. appease _____

   _____

8. decorum _____

   _____

9. suave _____

   _____

10. amenable _____

    _____

11. rueful _____

    _____

12. deference _____

    _____

Name: _____ Date: _____

Etiquette 4: *Sentences/Matching*

Directions: Complete each of the following sentences with the correct vocabulary word.

amenable	obliging	deference	boorish	hospitality

1. The man's behavior was _____; he was very ill-mannered.

2. Miguel was _____ to the idea of going to the movies.

3. Mrs. Delacruz offered the _____ of her home to the stranded motorists.

4. In _____ to Kim's broken arm, Kelly wrote two copies of the history notes.

5. We asked Spencer to help with the decorations, and he was _____.

Directions: Fill in the blank with the correct vocabulary word.

genteel	deference	suave	decorum
apropos	affable	rueful	appease

1. _____ yielding to the opinion of another out of respect for that person

2. _____ at the right time; fitting the occasion

3. _____ well-bred in polite society

4. _____ sophisticated

5. _____ friendly and easy to talk to

6. _____ dignified conduct

7. _____ showing regret

8. _____ to calm, especially by giving in to the demands of others

62

Science and Technology: *Vocabulary List*

In our changing world, new words are always being developed. Many of the new words, like *computer* and *microchip,* belong in the area of science and technology. Some of the words on this list have been around for hundreds of years, while some are only a few years old. In the next year and the years to come, more words will be invented and become part of our vocabulary. It is important to always be reading and learning these new words.

online	matter	density	hypothesis
experiment	theory	microchip	antibiotic
atom	barometer	zoology	paradigm
desktop	laptop	fusion	topography
loop	clinic	altimeter	centrifuge
results	obsolete	symbiosis	anthropology
diameter	conclusion	epidermis	capillary
biology	nutrient	physics	archaeology
fluid	kilometer	contagious	prognosis
corrode	geometry	contaminate	hypnotize
chemistry	window	norm	aqueduct
program	microbe	fission	phenomenon
	geology	petri dish	

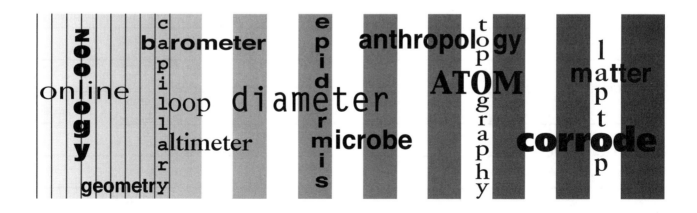

Name: _____ Date: _____

Science and Technology 1: *Definitions*

Directions: Use a dictionary to look up the definitions of the following science and technology words. Write a short definition, and then write a sentence that goes with the definition.

1. chemistry _____

   _____

2. online _____

   _____

3. program (computer) _____

   _____

4. corrode _____

   _____

5. experiment _____

   _____

6. fluid _____

   _____

7. atom _____

   _____

8. biology _____

   _____

9. desktop (computer) _____

   _____

10. diameter _____

    _____

11. results _____

    _____

12. loop (computer) _____

    _____

Name: _____ Date: _____

Science and Technology 1: *Sentences/Matching*

Directions: Complete each of the following sentences with the correct vocabulary word.

experiment   loop   diameters   online   corrode   biology

1. My computer program has a _____; it just keeps repeating.

2. The batteries are beginning to _____; they are leaking and are brown in places.

3. We had to measure the _____ of circles in math class.

4. My favorite part of science class is when we do an _____.

5. Clarissa said that in _____ they will be dissecting a frog.

6. Casey's mom told him he was too young to do _____ shopping on the computer.

Directions: Fill in the blank with the correct vocabulary word.

chemistry   atom   desktop   results   program   fluid

1. _____ something that is liquid

2. _____ the smallest part of an element

3. _____ a computer screen

4. _____ a series of commands given to a computer

5. _____ the science of the properties and composition of matter

6. _____ the conclusion of an experiment

If you could write a computer program, what would you have the computer do?

_____

_____

_____

Name: _____ Date: _____

Science and Technology 2: *Definitions*

Directions: Use a dictionary to look up the definitions of the following science and technology words. Write a short definition, and then write a sentence that goes with the definition.

1. matter _____

   _____

2. obsolete _____

   _____

3. conclusion _____

   _____

4. microbe _____

   _____

5. theory _____

   _____

6. geometry _____

   _____

7. barometer _____

   _____

8. clinic _____

   _____

9. geology _____

   _____

10. window (computer) _____

    _____

11. kilometer _____

    _____

12. laptop _____

    _____

13. nutrient _____

    _____

Name: _____ Date: _____

Science and Technology 2: *Sentences/Matching*

Directions: Complete each of the following sentences with the correct vocabulary word.

window   conclusion   microbe   barometer   obsolete   laptop

1. We looked at a tiny _____ under the microscope.

2. The _____ to our experiment showed us that water and oil don't mix.

3. My old computer is _____; it is too slow and doesn't have much memory.

4. Mario pulled down the menu to edit from the _____ on his desktop.

5. Steve wants a _____ to use to take notes in college.

6. Grandfather's _____ helps him forecast the weather for the day.

Directions: Fill in the blank with the correct vocabulary word.

nutrient   geometry   kilometer   matter
theory   geology   clinic

1. _____ a branch of math dealing with lines, angles, and shapes

2. _____ substance that makes up all physical objects

3. _____ a group of doctors' offices

4. _____ a possible explanation of why

5. _____ a substance that provides nourishment

6. _____ the study of rocks and minerals

7. _____ a metric measurement of length

Name: _____ Date: _____

Science and Technology 3: *Definitions*

Directions: Use a dictionary to look up the definitions of the following science and technology words. Write a short definition, and then write a sentence that goes with the definition.

1. contaminate _____

   _____

2. density _____

   _____

3. norm _____

   _____

4. microchip _____

   _____

5. fission _____

   _____

6. zoology _____

   _____

7. petri dish _____

   _____

8. fusion _____

   _____

9. contagious _____

   _____

10. altimeter _____

    _____

11. physics _____

    _____

12. symbiosis _____

    _____

13. epidermis _____

    _____

Name: _____ Date: _____

Science and Technology 3: *Sentences/Matching*

Directions: Complete each of the following sentences with the correct vocabulary word.

petri dish	**zoology**	**contaminate**	**contagious**
physics	**microchip**	**altimeter**	

1. Matt likes to be with animals, so he wants to study _____.

2. The _____ in the computer has many circuits.

3. Stan is going to study _____ because he is interested in force and motion.

4. Cover your mouth when you sneeze; those germs may be _____.

5. The pilot checked the _____ to see how high the plane was flying.

6. Keep your experiment covered; you don't want anything to _____ it.

7. Luanne is trying to grow mold in a _____.

Directions: Fill in the blank with the correct vocabulary word.

norm   density   symbiosis   epidermis   fusion   fission

1. _____ the relationship of two or more different organisms that live together

2. _____ splitting atoms into two parts

3. _____ the outer layer of the skin

4. _____ an average

5. _____ the amount that an area is filled with things or people

6. _____ melting things together with heat

Name: _____ Date: _____

Science and Technology 4: *Definitions*

Directions: Use a dictionary to look up the definitions of the following science and technology words. Write a short definition, and then write a sentence that goes with the definition.

1. phenomenon _____

   _____

2. hypnotize _____

   _____

3. aqueduct _____

   _____

4. hypothesis _____

   _____

5. capillary _____

   _____

6. paradigm _____

   _____

7. prognosis _____

   _____

8. antibiotic _____

   _____

9. centrifuge _____

   _____

10. archaeology _____

    _____

11. anthropology _____

    _____

12. topography _____

    _____

Name: _____ Date: _____

Science and Technology 4: *Sentences/Matching*

Directions: Complete each of the following sentences with the correct vocabulary word.

topography   aqueduct   antibiotic   hypothesis   archaeology   centrifuge

1. The _____ is the first step in a science project.

2. Mr. Meyer charts the terrain; he teaches _____.

3. Our science class used a _____ to separate the mixture.

4. In Roman times, the _____ was considered new technology.

5. Angela would like to go on a dig in Egypt; she is interested in _____.

6. Doctors won't give you an _____ for every illness.

Directions: Fill in the blank with the correct vocabulary word.

paradigm   capillary   prognosis   phenomenon   hypnotize   anthropology

1. _____ something that is exceptional

2. _____ a blood vessel

3. _____ a model

4. _____ the study of people and their cultures

5. _____ a prediction or forecast

6. _____ to put in a trance

What is your favorite science to study and why?

_____

_____

_____

_____

Consumer Management: *Vocabulary List*

There are certain words that are used in banking, the stock market, and other financial areas that are important to know. Some words are the same or similar to words that you have heard or read in other places, but they have a special meaning when associated with finances.

deposit	withdrawal	appraisal	pittance
bond	stock	beneficiary	notary public
portfolio	investment	validate	repository
securities	account	bankrupt	capital
overdraft	teller	destitute	economy
loan	mortgage	deduction	corporation
backlog	franchise	debt	endorse
barter	trade	contract	compensate
commerce	inflation	employee	deplete
vendor	merger	pension	compromise
inventory	monopoly	earnings	negotiate
transaction	payroll	interest	pact
	credit	retirement	

72

Name: _____ Date: _____

Consumer Management 1: *Definitions*

Directions: Use a dictionary to look up the definitions of the following consumer management words. Write a short definition, and then write a sentence that goes with the definition.

1. deposit _____

   _____

2. withdrawal _____

   _____

3. bond _____

   _____

4. stock _____

   _____

5. portfolio _____

   _____

6. investment _____

   _____

7. securities _____

   _____

8. account _____

   _____

9. overdraft _____

   _____

10. teller _____

    _____

11. loan _____

    _____

12. mortgage _____

    _____

Name: _____ Date: _____

Consumer Management 1: *Sentences/Matching*

Directions: Complete each of the following sentences with the correct vocabulary word.

loan   withdrawal   teller   account   deposit   stock

1. Beth is going to make a _____ from her savings account to buy a

   book.

2. I need a _____ of fifty cents to buy lunch today.

3. Fred's brother has a checking _____ at the local bank.

4. Mom makes a _____ at the bank on Friday when she gets paid.

5. Suzy works at the credit union; she is a _____ there.

6. In math, our teacher asked us to choose a _____ to watch and track

   its progress in the market.

Directions: Fill in the blank with the correct vocabulary word.

investment   bond   portfolio   mortgage   overdraft   securities

1. _____ a debt issued by a corporation

2. _____ stocks and bonds

3. _____ taking more out than is in a bank account

4. _____ a loan for a house

5. _____ securities and bonds owned by an individual

6. _____ money used for a profitable return

How much money would you like to save, and what would you save for?

_____

_____

_____

Name: _____ Date: _____

Consumer Management 2: *Definitions*

Directions: Use a dictionary to look up the definitions of the following consumer management words. Write a short definition, and then write a sentence that goes with the definition.

1. backlog _____

    _____

2. franchise _____

    _____

3. barter _____

    _____

4. trade _____

    _____

5. commerce _____

    _____

6. inflation _____

    _____

7. vendor _____

    _____

8. merger _____

    _____

9. inventory _____

    _____

10. monopoly _____

    _____

11. transaction _____

    _____

12. credit _____

    _____

13. payroll _____

    _____

Name: _____ Date: _____

Consumer Management 2: *Sentences/Matching*

Directions: Complete each of the following sentences with the correct vocabulary word.

inflation   transactions   commerce   vendor   credit   inventory   monopoly

1. _____ between states is important to our economy.

2. Chris was the only one selling water at the garage sale; he had a _____.

3. After she finished her _____ at the bank, Mom took us to get ice cream.

4. Ken asked the salesperson to check the _____ in the stockroom for

   the size shirt he was looking for.

5. Maria returned her sweater, and the clerk gave her a _____ instead

   of cash.

6. Last year gasoline was 99 cents; now it's over a dollar because of _____.

7. The hot dog _____ was busy during the lunch hour.

Directions: Fill in the blank with the correct vocabulary word.

franchise   backlog   trade   barter   merger   payroll

1. _____ a list of people who receive wages from a business

2. _____ the buying and selling of products

3. _____ the right to own a professional team or sell a product

4. _____ two or more companies joining together

5. _____ to trade goods or services without using money

6. _____ an accumulation of unfinished work

Name: _____ Date: _____

Consumer Management 3: *Definitions*

Directions: Use a dictionary to look up the definitions of the following consumer management words. Write a short definition and then write a sentence that goes with the definition.

1. destitute _____

   _____

2. deduction _____

   _____

3. validate _____

   _____

4. debt _____

   _____

5. appraisal _____

   _____

6. contract _____

   _____

7. employee _____

   _____

8. earnings _____

   _____

9. bankrupt _____

   _____

10. beneficiary _____

    _____

11. retirement _____

    _____

12. pension _____

    _____

13. interest _____

    _____

Name: _____ Date: _____

Consumer Management 3: *Sentences/Matching*

Directions: Complete each of the following sentences with the correct vocabulary word.

retirement	**debt**	**interest**	**contract**	**employee**	**pension**

1. Babette has a _____ with Julie; Babette owes her a dollar.

2. Mrs. Spencer said that we could make a _____ with her to get an "A."

3. My grandma and grandpa are enjoying their _____ in Arizona.

4. Sula's savings account is growing because of the _____ paid.

5. If you are an _____ at the grocery store, you must wear a uniform.

6. Often when you retire, you receive a _____ from the company.

Directions: Fill in the blank with the correct vocabulary word.

appraisal	**deduction**	**destitute**	**earnings**
validate	**bankrupt**	**beneficiary**	

1. _____ a sum or amount allowed to be subtracted

2. _____ lacking everything

3. _____ the salary of a person

4. _____ to confirm

5. _____ a valuation of something for sale

6. _____ having lost all your money and property

7. _____ a person who receives something from a will, insurance policy, etc.

If you had $10, what would you buy? If you had $100, what would you buy?

_____

_____

_____

_____

Name: _____ Date: _____

Consumer Management 4: *Definitions*

Directions: Use a dictionary to look up the definitions of the following consumer management words. Write a short definition, and then write a sentence that goes with the definition.

1. capital (financial) _____

   _____

2. corporation _____

   _____

3. pact _____

   _____

4. compensate _____

   _____

5. negotiate _____

   _____

6. pittance _____

   _____

7. compromise _____

   _____

8. notary public _____

   _____

9. deplete _____

   _____

10. repository _____

    _____

11. endorse _____

    _____

12. economy _____

    _____

Name: _____ Date: _____

Consumer Management 4: *Sentences/Matching/Short Answer*

Directions: Complete each of the following sentences with the correct vocabulary word.

capital   compromise   negotiate   endorse   pact   corporation

1. Dave needed his dad to invest some _____ into his project.

2. Jesse will need to _____ the check before depositing it in the bank.

3. Ann and Sue made a _____ not to talk about others.

4. The large _____ downtown has many offices.

5. A _____ was reached with the student council and the principal regarding the dress code.

6. George wanted to _____ with his parents for a later curfew.

Directions: Fill in the blank with the correct vocabulary word.

repository   economy   compensate   notary public   deplete   pittance

1. _____ to pay for something

2. _____ the resources of a country or state

3. _____ a person who validates documents

4. _____ to use up

5. _____ a place where things are stored

6. _____ a small share

Directions: Answer the following question.

1. Where might you find a **notary public**? _____

_____

Extra Vocabulary

A
ablaze
accessory
acute
adjourn
allergic
amiable
animate
arbitrate
aspiration
austere

D
daft
defendant
democratic
despite
destination
dinette
dominant
dread
drench
duress

G
gape
gargantuan
generator
genuine
glacial
gnaw
goad
graphic
guerrilla
gullible

J
jabber
jet stream
jingoism
jockey
joist
journalism
jovial
judicious
junta
justify

M
magnificent
manuscript
masquerade
melodious
merchant
metropolitan
mingle
monitor
monologue
mythology

B
babble
ballad
betray
bicameral
bizarre
blanch
boisterous
borough
bouquet
bureau

E
earthy
ecosphere
effective
elegant
emancipate
emit
encampment
enforce
epicurean
estimate

H
harsh
havoc
heredity
heroine
hoarse
hoax
horizontal
hostage
humility
hybrid

K
karaoke
keen
kerchief
ketch
kilt
kinetic
kinship
knoll
knuckle
kudos

N
necessitate
negate
nemesis
neutrality
nimble
noncommittal
nostalgia
notoriety
numerator
nurture

C
cameo
casualty
certify
clan
cleft
coarse
colossal
condone
crockery
cummerbund

F
famine
fanatic
finesse
fleet
flippant
flounder
forage
fragment
fray
functional

I
immune
impair
impartial
impolite
incumbent
index
inhabit
initialize
initiative
itinerary

L
laboratory
labyrinth
laudable
legible
legitimate
lenient
linear
logical
loiter
lucid

O
obligation
oblivious
obvious
occupational
official
olfactory
opaque
opener
ordeal
overture

Extra Vocabulary

P
packet
panacea
pedestrian
philosophy
picket
plagiarize
potent
probable
proliferate
purge

S
saturation
scrutinize
scurry
sediment
shard
significant
skirmish
stipend
supposition
symmetry

V
vacate
vague
veneer
verbose
vibrant
visualize
volatile
volunteer
vouch
vulgar

Y
yammer
yawn
yearning
yeoman
yield
yodel
yonder
youngster
yowl
Yukon

Q
quagmire
quaint
quandary
quark
quarrel
quell
quill
quip
quorum
quote

T
tangible
tantalize
telecommunication
terminology
thwart
tilt
totalitarian
traverse
treacherous
tutorial

W
waft
waiver
wearable
wedge
wharf
witness
woeful
wonderment
wrack
wrought

Z
zany
zealot
zenith
zephyr
zeppelin
zest
zilch
zinc
zither
zodiac

R
radiant
rarity
redeem
rejuvenate
reproach
retaliate
ridiculous
righteous
rogue
ruinous

U
ultimate
umbrage
unanimous
universal
upshot
urbane
usable
utilitarian
utmost
utterance

X
xanthic
xebec
xenolith
xenon
xenophobia
xeric
xiphoid
xylem
xyloid
xyster

Answer Keys

Occupations and Careers 1: Matching (p. 4)

1. farmer
2. police officer
3. salesperson
4. lawyer
5. nurse
6. doctor
7. engineer
8. secretary
9. dentist
10. reporter
11. chef
12. teacher
13. forest ranger

Occupations and Careers 1: Sentences (p. 5)

1. teacher
2. salesperson
3. police officer
4. doctor
5. secretary
6. chef
7. lawyer
8. forest ranger
9. reporter
10. nurse
11. farmer
12. engineer
13. dentist

Occupations and Careers 2: Matching (p. 6)

1. accountant
2. firefighter
3. gardener
4. waiter
5. pilot
6. nanny
7. principal
8. sailor
9. diva
10. waitress
11. executive
12. mechanic

Occupations and Careers 2: Sentences (p. 7)

1. nanny
2. mechanic
3. executives
4. accountant
5. principal
6. waiter
7. firefighter
8. pilot
9. diva
10. sailor
11. gardener
12. waitress

Occupations and Careers 3: Definitions (p. 8)

1. ecologist: a person who studies organisms and their environments
2. computer programmer: a person who writes instructions for a computer
3. dental hygienist: a professional who cleans teeth
4. veterinarian: a doctor who treats animals
5. physician: a doctor of medicine
6. cartographer: a person who draws maps
7. geologist: a person who studies rocks
8. architect: a person who designs buildings
9. psychiatrist: a doctor who deals with mental disorders
10. maitre d': a headwaiter
11. actor: a person who plays a character in a movie or play
12. stockbroker: a person who buys and sells stocks for investors

Occupations and Careers 3: Sentences (p. 9)

1. veterinarian
2. actor
3. psychiatrist
4. dental hygienists
5. geologist
6. cartographer
7. ecologist
8. computer programmer
9. physician
10. maitre d'
11. Stockbrokers
12. architect

Occupations and Careers 4: Definitions (p. 10)

1. computerist: a person who uses and operates a computer
2. surgeon: a doctor who specializes in surgery
3. mathematician: a specialist who deals with mathematics
4. construction worker: a person who builds houses, buildings, roads, etc.
5. undertaker: a person who arranges funerals
6. optometrist: a doctor who takes care of people's eyes
7. vendor: a person who sells things
8. professor: a faculty member at a college or university

Answer Keys

9. photographer: a person who takes pictures with a camera
10. decorator: a person who designs the interiors of homes, offices, etc.
11. pharmacist: a person who dispenses prescription medicines
12. artisan: a craftsperson
13. auctioneer: a person who sells things at an auction

Occupations and Careers 4: Sentences (p. 11)

1. mathematician
2. professor
3. undertaker
4. photographer
5. computerist
6. surgeon
7. vendors
8. artisans
9. auctioneer
10. pharmacist
11. optometrist
12. decorator
13. construction workers

Occupations and Careers: Word Search (p. 12)

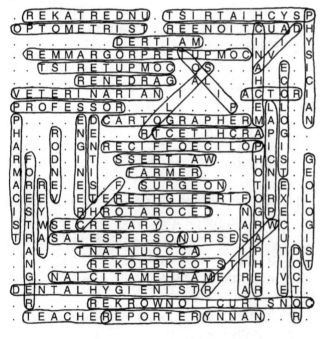

Character Building 1: Definitions (p. 14)

1. loyalty: the quality of being faithful to someone or some idea
2. responsibility: the quality of being accountable
3. polite: having and showing good manners
4. personality: behavior and emotional characteristics
5. respect: to hold in high esteem
6. mannerly: using good manners
7. optimism: being positive in attitude
8. confidence: trust
9. trustworthy: deserving of someone's trust
10. fortitude: courage and strength in emotions
11. honest: truthful
12. caring: to be concerned about; take care of

Character Building 1: Sentences (p. 15)

1. respect
2. confidence
3. responsibility
4. honest
5. caring
6. polite

Character Building 2: Definitions (p. 16)

1. vigor: to have good physical and mental health
2. championship: contest to declare the best
3. humane: tender, caring, compassionate
4. kindness: the quality of being good and gentle
5. resourceful: able to deal promptly and effectively with problems
6. reputation: the way a person is thought of
7. creative: inventive; imaginative
8. sociable: friendly
9. careful: cautious
10. dependable: worthy of respect and trust
11. graceful: elegant in motion
12. civil: polite, often in a formal manner
13. concern: worry about someone

84

Answer Keys

Character Building 2: Sentences (p. 17)
1. careful   2. kindness
3. championship   4. Humane
5. reputation   6. concern
7. sociable

Character Building 3: Definitions (p. 18)
1. tireless: unable to be exhausted
2. esteem: to respect or hold in high regard
3. aristocratic: noble
4. compassion: sympathy shown to someone
5. discerning: to show good judgment
6. hospitable: treating guests favorably
7. reason: showing sound judgment
8. attentive: being concerned about someone or something
9. visionary: a person who has new ideas
10. conviction: a strong belief
11. competency: the ability to do something in a capable manner
12. attribute: a specific characteristic
13. temperament: the emotional attitude of a person

Character Building 3: Matching (p. 19)
1. visionary   2. esteem
3. conviction   4. aristocratic
5. temperament   6. hospitable

Character Building 4: Definitions (p. 20)
1. insightful: being able to see intuitively
2. attitude: expression of someone through posture or actions
3. persuasive: able to convince or sway someone's opinion
4. genial: cheerful; pleasant
5. adaptable: able to change and fit in
6. integrity: honesty in what one does
7. resolute: determined
8. distinguished: elegant in appearance
9. gallant: polite
10. propriety: following standards of proper

behavior and good manners
11. ethical: in accordance with rules and laws
12. experienced: skillful

Character Building 4: Sentences (p. 21)
1. distinguished   2. attitude
3. persuasive   4. genial
5. resolute

Character Building 4: Short Answers (p. 21)
1. no   2. no

Character Building: Crossword Puzzle (p. 22)

Everyday Words 1: Definitions (p. 24)
1. composite: made up of different parts
2. refuse: garbage; trash
3. remote: distant
4. enviable: something to be envied
5. biopsy: a body tissue sample taken to test for disease
6. disheveled: untidy in appearance; unkempt
7. impromptu: without practice
8. academic: pertaining to education or learning
9. dowdy: not stylish; old-fashioned in dress
10. align: to put in order or in a line
11. fervor: great zest or excitement
12. apparatus: equipment used for a specific job or sport

85

Answer Keys

Everyday Words 1: Matching (p. 25)
1. composite
2. dowdy
3. refuse
4. enviable
5. academic
6. biopsy

Everyday Words 1: Short Answers (p. 25)
1. yes
2. no
3. no
4. yes
5. no
6. no

Everyday Words 2: Definitions (p. 26)
1. situation: location or position
2. linger: to remain behind
3. escort: to accompany
4. delegate: someone who represents someone else
5. resource: supplies or natural elements to be used
6. adept: to be skilled
7. ecological: dealing with the environment and its protection
8. commence: to begin
9. fertile: productive
10. junction: intersection
11. terrarium: a glass jar or bowl with small plants and/or animals living inside
12. shun: to avoid
13. seminar: students studying a subject in a small group

Everyday Words 2: Sentences (p. 27)
1. shun
2. seminar
3. terrarium
4. fertile
5. ecological
6. resource
7. escort

Everyday Words 2: Matching (p. 27)
1. situation
2. delegate
3. linger
4. adept
5. commence
6. junction

Everyday Words 2: Short Answers (p. 27)
1. yes
2. no

Everyday Words 3: Definitions (p. 28)
1. candor: direct honesty
2. environment: surroundings
3. paraphrase: to rephrase for easier understanding
4. colleague: a person who works with you
5. orchestrate: to lead or organize
6. zealous: extremely enthusiastic; fervent
7. meander: wander
8. jubilant: overjoyed; elated
9. inhumane: lacking compassion
10. calligraphy: fancy, decorative writing
11. eloquent: having fluent, persuasive speech or writing
12. extemporaneous: without rehearsal
13. debonair: well-dressed

Everyday Words 3: Matching (p. 29)
1. environment
2. calligraphy
3. inhumane
4. orchestrate
5. paraphrase
6. debonair

Everyday Words 3: Short Answers (p. 29)
1. no
2. yes

Everyday Words 4: Definitions (p. 30)
1. saunter: to walk leisurely
2. beneficial: advantageous; helpful
3. judicial: fair; impartial
4. rampage: an outbreak of violent, raging behavior
5. frugal: penny-pinching; careful with money
6. negligible: a very small amount
7. complacent: satisfied; smug
8. personable: agreeable
9. prudent: careful
10. arbitrary: not fixed by rules, but left to one's judgment
11. jargon: words used for a specific purpose
12. retort: a sharp reply

Answer Keys

Everyday Words 4: Sentences (p. 31)
1. retort
2. rampage
3. frugal
4. beneficial
5. negligible
6. complacent

Everyday Words 4: Short Answers (p. 31)
1. no
2. yes

Words to Enrich Writing 1: Definitions (p. 33)
1. shimmer: to reflect light
2. elated: filled with great happiness
3. encroach: to gradually move forward
4. unusual: not ordinary
5. important: held in high regard
6. colorful: having many or bright colors
7. sadness: unhappiness
8. hopeless: desperate
9. uneventful: ordinary; routine
10. gloomy: dark; dreary
11. excited: having one's feelings or passions aroused
12. shy: bashful

Words to Enrich Writing 1: Matching (p. 34)
1. encroach
2. shimmer
3. excited
4. hopeless
5. uneventful
6. sadness

Words to Enrich Writing 2: Definitions (p. 35)
1. sparkle: shine
2. alleged: asserted without any proof
3. impeccable: perfect
4. impressive: having a strong effect on the mind or emotions
5. constrained: unnatural; stiff
6. enjoyable: pleasant to be with or to do
7. pale: light in color
8. sorrowful: sad
9. enormous: huge
10. reserved: quiet; shy
11. radiant: glowing
12. awkward: clumsy
13. trying: difficult to deal with

Words to Enrich Writing 2: Sentences (p. 36)
1. reserved
2. pale
3. sparkled
4. impressive
5. trying
6. alleged

Words to Enrich Writing 3: Definitions (p. 37)
1. evict: to turn someone out
2. opportunity: a good chance or occasion
3. allude: to refer to indirectly
4. temporary: not permanent
5. squander: waste
6. clarify: to make something clearer
7. habitat: a natural environment
8. eloquence: skill in speech or writing
9. vivacious: animated; lively
10. reluctant: unwilling; holding back
11. momentary: not lasting very long
12. bellow: a roar
13. enlighten: to explain thoroughly; to make aware of

Words to Enrich Writing 3: Sentences (p. 38)
1. temporary
2. evict
3. opportunity
4. squander
5. enlighten
6. momentary

Words to Enrich Writing 3: Matching (p. 38)
1. bellow
2. clarify
3. eloquence
4. allude
5. vivacious
6. reluctant
7. habitat

Words to Enrich Writing 4: Definitions (p. 39)
1. overjoyed: excited; jubilant
2. multitude: a large group
3. desire: want
4. somber: serious

Answer Keys

5. elaboration: a more thorough explanation
6. deteriorate: to decay
7. fictitious: from one's imagination; not true
8. browse: to look at
9. generality: a general statement; not specific
10. imminent: likely to happen without delay
11. inclination: a tendency to do or say something
12. extinguish: to put out

Words to Enrich Writing 4: Short Answers (p. 40)

1. no	2. yes
3. no	4. no
5. yes	6. yes
7. yes	8. no

Recreation and Fitness 1: Definitions (p. 43)

1. crunch: to compress, as in a sit-up
2. accelerate: to increase the speed
3. ace: to make one point (tennis) or a hole-in-one (golf)
4. bunker: a sand trap or other barren hazard on a golf course
5. blocking: to keep an opponent from progressing, as in basketball or football
6. agility: ability to move quickly
7. target: the goal to be reached; an area aimed at
8. penalty: punishment given for a foul
9. dunk: to leap up and thrust the ball down into the basket in the game of basketball
10. coach: a person who instructs a team or individual athletes
11. angler: a fisherman
12. quiver: a bag to keep arrows in
13. fumble: to drop the ball

Recreation and Fitness 2: Definitions (p. 45)

1. court: level area used for sports such as basketball, tennis, or racquetball
2. marathon: a 26-mile-long race
3. foul: against the rules of the game
4. endurance: ability to continue despite fatigue
5. goal post: supports a crossbar to form a goal
6. fitness: health
7. barbell: a rod with adjustable weights on the ends
8. carbohydrate: starch or sugar important to humans
9. triathlete: a person who competes in swimming, biking, and running
10. badminton: game using a net, racket, and shuttlecock
11. croquet: lawn game with wickets, mallets, and balls
12. backboard: the area to which a basketball hoop is attached

Recreation and Fitness 2: Matching (p. 46)

1.	backboard	2.	marathon
3.	triathlete	4.	badminton
5.	court	6.	carbohydrates
7.	foul	8.	croquet
9.	goal post	10.	barbell
11.	fitness	12.	endurance

Recreation and Fitness 2: Short Answers (p. 47)

1. no	2. yes
3. no	4. no
5. yes	6. no
7. no	8. no
9. no	10. no

Recreation and Fitness 3: Definitions (p. 48)

1. philatelist: stamp collector
2. referee: a person who officiates at a game
3. embroidery: stitches used to decorate fabric, usually with colored thread

Answer Keys

4. arena: a large area used for sports
5. stamina: the power to keep going
6. competition: a contest between teams or people
7. wellness: the study of health and healthful things
8. curling: a game played on ice with brooms and a large stone
9. woodworking: to work with wood to build or for decoration
10. tournament: a competition between several teams
11. vascular: having to do with the heart and bloodstream
12. spectator: someone who watches a sporting event

Recreation and Fitness 3: Sentences (p. 49)
1. woodworking
2. philatelist
3. embroidery
4. wellness
5. curling
6. vascular

Recreation and Fitness 3: Matching (p. 50)
1. vascular
2. wellness
3. referee
4. embroidery
5. curling
6. arena
7. competition
8. woodworking
9. stamina
10. spectator
11. tournament
12. philatelist

Recreation and Fitness 4: Definitions (p. 51)
1. terpsichorean: related to dancing; a dancer
2. aerobics: exercises that condition the heart and lungs by increasing the efficiency of oxygen intake
3. offense: the part of the team responsible for scoring
4. gymnast: a person who performs tumbling and acrobatic exercises on special equipment
5. avocation: a hobby
6. treadmill: a machine to use for walking exercise

7. prestidigitation: magic tricks; sleight of hand
8. defense: the part of the team meant to stop the offense from scoring
9. aviation: flying
10. craft: to make something from wood, cloth, etc.
11. Olympian: one who participates in the Olympic games
12. league: an association of several teams
13. skeletal: referring to the bone system

Recreation and Fitness 4: Sentences (p. 52)
1. prestidigitation
2. Olympian
3. treadmill
4. offense
5. aerobics
6. terpsichorean

Etiquette 1: Definitions (p. 54)
1. apologize: to make an excuse for
2. tribute: a compliment given as respect or admiration
3. socialite: an important person in fashionable society
4. arrogance: overbearing pride or self-importance
5. manners: the polite ways of social behavior
6. respond: to answer; reply
7. invitation: a written or spoken request
8. thank you: an expression of gratitude
9. belated: coming late
10. respectful: showing politeness
11. compliment: statement of praise
12. social: a party; having to do with society
13. formal: dressier than everyday clothes

Etiquette 1: Matching (p. 55)
1. thank you
2. respectful
3. formal
4. apologize
5. invitation
6. manners
7. tribute
8. socialite
9. compliment
10. belated
11. respond
12. social
13. arrogance

Answer Keys

Etiquette 2: Definitions (p. 56)
1. politely: in a considerate manner
2. correctness: proper behavior
3. culture: refinement of the intellect, manners, and taste
4. please: a polite request
5. appreciation: thankfulness
6. diplomatic: being able to deal with difficult situations
7. nicety: the quality of being nice; something dainty or elegant
8. encouragement: expression of support and praise for someone
9. gracious: kind and courteous to guests
10. curtsy: a gesture or greeting of respect done by a bending of the knees and a slight lowering of the body
11. thoughtful: being considerate
12. valiant: brave
13. courteous: showing good manners; polite

Etiquette 2: Sentences (p. 57)
1. incorrect   2. correct
3. incorrect   4. correct
5. correct   6. correct
7. correct   8. incorrect
9. incorrect   10. correct
11. Mr. President or President _____
12. Governor _____

Etiquette 2: Sentences (p. 58)
1. Please   2. appreciation
3. diplomatic   4. politely
5. curtsy

Etiquette 2: Matching (p. 58)
1. correctness   2. encouragement
3. thoughtful   4. culture

Etiquette 3: Definitions (p. 59)
1. RSVP: abbreviation for the French phrase *réspondez s'il vous plaît,* which means "respond, if you please"

2. cordial: gracious; polite
3. tact: knowing what to say to avoid offending someone
4. homage: to pay respect to
5. belligerent: aggressive; angry
6. debutante: a young girl making her first public appearance in society
7. dignity: self-respect
8. remorseful: full of regret
9. chivalrous: courteous to women and girls
10. aplomb: poise and self-possession
11. benevolent: being kind and generous
12. refinement: elegant taste

Etiquette 3: Sentences (p. 60)
1. cordial   2. belligerent
3. benevolent   4. refinement
5. RSVP

Etiquette 3: Matching (p. 60)
1. chivalrous   2. aplomb
3. remorseful   4. tact
5. dignity   6. homage
7. debutante   8. RSVP

Etiquette 4: Definitions (p. 61)
1. hospitality: the act of being hospitable; generous entertainment of guests
2. obliging: willing to help out
3. affable: friendly and easy to talk to
4. apropos: at the right time; fitting the occasion
5. genteel: well-bred in polite society
6. boorish: rude
7. appease: to calm, especially by giving in to the demands of others
8. decorum: dignified conduct
9. suave: sophisticated
10. amenable: agreeable
11. rueful: showing regret
12. deference: yielding to the opinion of another out of respect for that person

Answer Keys

Etiquette 4: Sentences (p. 62)
1. boorish   2. amenable
3. hospitality   4. deference
5. obliging

Etiquette 4: Matching (p. 62)
1. deference   2. apropos
3. genteel   4. suave
5. affable   6. decorum
7. rueful   8. appease

Science and Technology 1: Definitions (p. 64)
1. chemistry: the science of the composition and properties of matter
2. online: being hooked up to the main computer or Internet
3. program: a series of commands given to a computer
4. corrode: to wear away
5. experiment: a procedure to test a hypothesis
6. fluid: something that is liquid
7. atom: the smallest part of an element
8. biology: the science of living matter
9. desktop: the computer screen
10. diameter: the measurement across a circle from one side to the other, passing through the center of the circle
11. results: the conclusion of an experiment
12. loop: a place in a program where the action is repeating

Science and Technology 1: Sentences (p. 65)
1. loop   2. corrode
3. diameters   4. experiment
5. biology   6. online

Science and Technology 1: Matching (p. 65)
1. fluid   2. atom
3. desktop   4. program
5. chemistry   6. results

Science and Technology 2: Definitions (p. 66)
1. matter: the substance that makes up all physical objects
2. obsolete: out of style or practice
3. conclusion: the results of an experiment
4. microbe: a small organism
5. theory: a possible explanation of why
6. geometry: a branch of mathematics that deals with lines, angles, and shapes
7. barometer: an instrument to measure atmospheric pressure
8. clinic: a small group of doctors' offices
9. geology: the study of rocks and minerals
10. window: an option on the desktop to allow users to access other areas
11. kilometer: a metric measurement of length
12. laptop: a small portable computer
13. nutrient: a substance that provides nourishment

Science and Technology 2: Sentences (p. 67)
1. microbe   2. conclusion
3. obsolete   4. window
5. laptop   6. barometer

Science and Technology 2: Matching (p. 67)
1. geometry   2. matter
3. clinic   4. theory
5. nutrient   6. geology
7. kilometer

Answer Keys

Science and Technology 3: Definitions (p. 68)

1. contaminate: to pollute
2. density: the amount that an area is filled with things or people
3. norm: an average
4. microchip: a small chip with circuits on it
5. fission: splitting atoms into two parts
6. zoology: the study of animals
7. petri dish: a small glass dish used for experiments
8. fusion: melting things together with heat
9. contagious: infections that can be transmitted
10. altimeter: an instrument on an airplane to show altitude
11. physics: the study of force and motion
12. symbiosis: the relationship of two or more different organisms that live together
13. epidermis: the outer layer of the skin

Science and Technology 3: Sentences (p. 69)

1. zoology
2. microchip
3. physics
4. contagious
5. altimeter
6. contaminate
7. petri dish

Science and Technology 3: Matching (p. 69)

1. symbiosis
2. fission
3. epidermis
4. norm
5. density
6. fusion

Science and Technology 4: Definitions (p. 70)

1. phenomenon: something that is exceptional
2. hypnotize: to put in a trance
3. aqueduct: a channel to carry water
4. hypothesis: a theory for an experiment
5. capillary: a blood vessel
6. paradigm: a model
7. prognosis: a prediction or forecast
8. antibiotic: a medicine to kill bacteria
9. centrifuge: a piece of equipment that spins at high speed
10. archaeology: the study of the life and culture of past, especially ancient, people through excavation of ancient sites and artifacts
11. anthropology: the study of people and their cultures
12. topography: the study of the land in a specific area

Science and Technology 4: Sentences (p. 71)

1. hypothesis
2. topography
3. centrifuge
4. aqueduct
5. archaeology
6. antibiotic

Science and Technology 4: Matching (p. 71)

1. phenomenon
2. capillary
3. paradigm
4. anthropology
5. prognosis
6. hypnotize

Consumer Management 1: Definitions (p. 73)

1. deposit: putting money into a bank account
2. withdrawal: taking money out of a bank account
3. bond: a debt issued by a corporation
4. stock: a share in a company
5. portfolio: securities and bonds owned by an individual
6. investment: money used for a profitable return
7. securities: stocks and bonds
8. account: an amount of money deposited in a bank
9. overdraft: taking more out than is in a bank account

Answer Keys

10. teller: a person employed by a bank to work at the counter
11. loan: money borrowed to be paid back
12. mortgage: a loan for a house

Consumer Management 1: Sentences (p. 74)

1. withdrawal	2. loan
3. account	4. deposit
5. teller	6. stock

Consumer Management 1: Matching (p. 74)

1. bond	2. securities
3. overdraft	4. mortgage
5. portfolio	6. investment

Consumer Management 2: Definitions (p. 75)

1. backlog: an accumulation of unfinished work
2. franchise: the right to own a professional sports team or to sell a product
3. barter: to exchange goods or services without using money
4. trade: the buying and selling of products
5. commerce: exchanging goods between states and countries
6. inflation: when money becomes devalued because of a rise in prices
7. vendor: someone who sells something
8. merger: two or more companies joining together
9. inventory: merchandise kept on hand to sell
10. monopoly: total control over a business or product
11. transaction: the exchange of money for a product; the conducting of business
12. credit: allowing someone to pay for goods or services later; a sum of money in an account on which a person can draw
13. payroll: a list of people who receive wages

Consumer Management 2: Sentences (p. 76)

1. Commerce	2. monopoly
3. transactions	4. inventory
5. credit	6. inflation
7. vendor	

Consumer Management 2: Matching (p. 76)

1. payroll	2. trade
3. franchise	4. merger
5. barter	6. backlog

Consumer Management 3: Definitions (p. 77)

1. destitute: lacking in everything
2. deduction: a sum or amount allowed to be subtracted
3. validate: to confirm
4. debt: something owed to someone
5. appraisal: valuation of something for sale
6. contract: an agreement between two or more people, especially when written
7. employee: someone who works for someone else
8. earnings: the salary of a person
9. bankrupt: having lost all money and property
10. beneficiary: a person who receives something from a will, insurance policy, etc.
11. retirement: leaving a job at a certain age
12. pension: money received during retirement
13. interest: money earned on deposits in savings plans

Consumer Management 3: Sentences (p. 78)

1. debt	2. contract
3. retirement	4. interest
5. employee	6. pension

Answer Keys

Consumer Management 3: Matching (p. 78)

1. deduction
2. destitute
3. earnings
4. validate
5. appraisal
6. bankrupt
7. beneficiary

Consumer Management 4: Definitions (p. 79)

1. capital: money used to invest
2. corporation: a business that is a legal entity
3. pact: a promise between people or companies
4. compensate: to pay for something
5. negotiate: to bargain with someone
6. pittance: a small share
7. compromise: an agreement where each side agrees to give up something
8. notary public: a person who validates documents
9. deplete: to use up
10. repository: a place where things are stored
11. endorse: to sign the back of a check for deposit
12. economy: the resources of a country or state

Consumer Management 4: Sentences (p. 80)

1. capital
2. endorse
3. pact
4. corporation
5. compromise
6. negotiate

Consumer Management 4: Matching (p. 80)

1. compensate
2. economy
3. notary public
4. deplete
5. repository
6. pittance

Consumer Management 4: Short Answer (p. 80)

1. In a bank, at a courthouse, etc.